What people are saying about 'Not the Bible'

If I were alive today, I would be happy to condemn these parables as heretical.

Martin Luther*

'Awesome. Excellent. Recommended' are some adjectives I found in the thesaurus. However I wouldn't use any of them to describe this book.

Dick Shunnary

This is fake good news!

Donald Trump*

When I read 'Not the Bible' I feel the pleasure of God.

Eric Liddle's sixth cousin twice removed*

---

* Everything's true about these statements except the quotes.

N🚫T
THE PARABLES
OF JESUS

Other books by the author

The Lost Parables Series

The Donkey and the King

Ana and the Prince

Forthcoming Not the Bible Titles

More Not the Parables of Jesus

Yet More Not the Parables of Jesus

Not the Christmas Story

Forthcoming Satirical Publishing Titles

How I sold 12 books in 2 years

N**O**T
THE PARABLES
OF **JESUS**

REVISED SATIRICAL VERSION (RSV)

John Spencer

Published by:

Kingdom Collective Publishing

Unit 10936, PO Box 6945
London, W1A 6US
kingdomcollectivepublishing@gmail.com

Book and Cover idea by John Lee, design by Akira007
The Not the Bible icon – design by John Lee, created by dalmatirac design studio
Editing by Katherine Walden.
ISBN: 978-1-912045-63-1
Printed and bound in Great Britain by Marston Book Services Ltd, Oxfordshire
First Edition: October 2017

Dedication

This one's for Dave Perry, former Dean of Theology at King's Bible College.

Thank you for giving me a greater love for Scripture and encouraging me to dig deeper.

Thank you for also appreciating my humour (especially Dave Perryingo and the Spider-Dave comic).

May you stick these parables in your theological pipe and smoke them long and hard.

CONTENTS

N⊘T
the End

A clever section title that makes it sound like it's more important than an introduction.

Hopefully, people might read it which may cut down on the number of angry emails I receive...

Why "Not the Parables"?
The Heart Behind the Series

Sometimes we can become overfamiliar with the Bible and lose sight of the impact and wonder that the parables first had on us. Worse yet, we can switch our hearts off, skim read, and miss what God wants to say to us through them today.

The aim of these different takes on the parables is to snap us out of our overfamiliarity and open our eyes to the truth of the Gospel.

They are half tongue-in-cheek and half right between the eyes.

May these "Not the Parables of Jesus" reawaken the wonder and joy, speak truth to your heart, and open your eyes to any cultural bias, hidden assumptions and other lies that may have crept in unawares.

Why use parables?

Then Jesus went out of the house, and sat by the lake. Such large crowds gathered round him that he got into a boat and sat in it, while all the people stood on the shore. Then he taught them the parable of the sower in *plain* language:

"When you hear God speaking there will likely be one of four responses:

"Some of you will shut your mind to the truth because you're blinded by prejudice, or you're unteachable due to your pride.

"Some of you will have an emotional experience, but when things get hard, and you don't 'feel it' anymore then you'll give up on God as it's not 'working for you.'

"Some of you will respond to God, but your career, your family, your social media and frankly anything else will leave no room for him.

"But some of you will receive it, nurture it, and see it grow in your life and produce fruit."

The disciples came to him and asked, "Why do you speak to the people in such plain language?"

Jesus replied, "I speak this way because facts are so engaging and move the heart far more than any story ever could. Besides they are more memorable and have the added benefit of spoon-feeding people truth rather than having them seek after it themselves.

"Don't ask, as it will be given to you anyway, don't bother seeking, as it will drop into your lap, and the whole knocking thing is completely unnecessary, as I have set before you an open door*."

---

* Yes I know I could have just told you the reason why I'm using parables to teach truth – but the whole point is that a story reaches places that a statement doesn't.

A note on spelling

I am British, and therefore, I use the Queen's English throughout this book.

However, there are some people in the world who rebelled against the sovereignty of my country[†]. They then went one step further and changed the spelling of our common language; having the audacity to continue to call their version 'English.'

Know that I am praying that they would, like the prodigal son, repent of their evil spelling ways and return home.

---

† I'm naming no names but you know who you are.

N⊘T
the Parables

Different takes on the parables to restore the wonder, the joy of the Gospel and the discomfort of discovering what we really believe in our hearts.

Parable of the Sower

A farmer was sowing seed. As he scattered the seed, some fell along the path, and the birds ate it. The farmer didn't shoo the birds but shouted at the seed, 'Why did you let yourself get eaten?!'

Some fell on rocky soil where it sprouted quickly. Because it didn't put down roots it withered and died in the sun. The farmer didn't remove the rocks but shouted at the seeds for not putting down deep enough roots.

Other seeds fell among weeds that choked the plants. The farmer didn't remove the weeds but blamed the seeds for not being fully devoted to growth.

Some seeds fell on good soil and produced a fantastic crop. The farmer praised them, 'Well done! You worked hard, and that's why you grew so much more than all the other seeds.'

Whoever has a mouth, criticise those that don't do well!

The Lamp on a Stand

No one lights a lamp and then hides it under a basket or a bowl. Unless, of course, your light is offensive to the darkness. In that case, you should keep your light private. Don't use it to show something contrary to the world's darkness, lest you offend anyone.

Parable of the Mustard Seed

The Kingdom of Heaven is like a magic mustard seed that when planted in the ground, it instantly becomes a fully grown plant. So too will you become perfect and mature with a fully developed godly character the moment you are saved.

The Hidden Treasure

The kingdom of Heaven is like treasure buried in a field. A man was so busy scrolling through his Instagram feed that he walked right over it without ever knowing of its existence. However, he did see some great memes that made him laugh.

Parable of the Net

The Kingdom of Heaven is like a man who cast a net into the sea. The net gathered all kinds of things. The man was so shocked to discover some useless things inside the net that he tossed it aside and vowed never to go fishing again.

So too will people discover that the church is not perfect then curse it and have nothing to do with it ever again.

The Unforgiving Servant

Then Peter came to Jesus and asked, "Master, how many times should I forgive my brother Andrew who sins against me? The other rabbis say only three times but seeing as you are more holy than the rest, should it be seven times, the number of perfection?"

Jesus replied, "Not bad Peter, obviously you can't be more gracious than God, but if you want to be seen as truly magnificent, aim for seventy-seven times."

So, Peter whittled a "sin stick" and marked it every time he forgave Andrew, knowing that once he had forgiven his brother exactly seventy-seven times, he would be considered very holy. He could then rightfully hold on to all grudges after that.

Jesus told them this parable: "The Kingdom of Heaven is like a king who decided to settle accounts with his servants. One of his servants who was brought before him owed seven billion dollars.

"He couldn't possibly pay it back, so the king ordered the man, his wife, children, and all his belongings to be sold to repay the debt.

"The man threw himself at the king's feet and begged, 'Be patient with me, and I'll pay it all back.' The king took pity on him, released him, and forgave all his debt.

"After the man had left the king's chamber, he came upon one of his fellow servants who owed him 12,000 dollars. He grabbed his fellow servant by the throat and demanded, 'Pay back what you owe me!'

"His fellow servant begged, 'Be patient with me and I'll pay it all back.' The man would have done so had the fellow servant thrown himself at his feet in the same way he had prostrated himself before the king. However, since his fellow servant didn't take on the same posture, it was clear the apology was faulty. Therefore, he had the servant put in jail until the debt was repaid in full. When the other servants saw this, they were outraged and told the king everything.

"The king summoned the man and said, 'Well done good and faithful servant! You really know how to judge others as inferior to yourself and undeserving of your mercy. Keep up the excellent legalistic work.'

"So too shall my Heavenly Father treat you if you follow the letter of the law exactly."

The Good Samaritan

Jesus replied, "There once was a man travelling from Jerusalem to Jericho who was attacked by robbers. But the man had made sure he was armed, thus ensuring he didn't need to rely on anyone else. And so, he beat off his attackers through his own strength.

"A priest happened to be going down the same road, but there was no need to help the man. So too, a Levite and a Samaritan came along, but neither of these was needed either.

"Which of these would you say was the most self-sufficient?"

The expert in the law replied, "The man who was attacked."

Jesus replied, "Go and do likewise."

The Lost Sheep

What do you think? If a man has one hundred sheep and ninety-nine of them wander away but the prize ram remains, will that man not be grateful that he still has the most prized one? Will he not rejoice over this one ram and not bother to go after the others who wandered off?

So it is with God, who doesn't mind if a congregation is lost as long as his prized megachurch pastor is kept.

The Prodigal Son

A man had two sons. The younger said to his father, 'Father, give me my share of the estate now, instead of making me wait until you die.' The Father replied, 'You're joking, right? I'm not going to give you anything, you ungrateful child!' And he locked him in his room forever.

The Lost Coin

Suppose a woman has ten silver coins and loses one. Won't she light a lamp, sweep the house and search every corner of the house until she finds the coin? And when she finds it, won't she call her friends and neighbours to rejoice with her? And won't her friends and neighbours look at her incredulously and say, 'It's only a coin, it's really not worth celebrating.'

In the same way, God's not that worried about finding the lost as there's already plenty of people in heaven worshipping him. What's one more to Him? After all, he could always make the rocks praise him if He finds himself short of worshipers.

The Shrewd Manager

Jesus told this story to his disciples, "There was a rich man who had a manager who handled his affairs. However, he heard reports that the manager was lining his own pockets. So he summoned him and asked, 'What's this I hear about you? You're sacked, and I want a complete audit of your books.'

"The manager said to himself, 'What am I to do now? I'm not strong enough for manual labour, and I'm too proud to beg. Wait! I know what to do! I'll change the accounts to pin the blame on somebody else so that I can keep my job.'

"His master had to admire the crooked manager for his deviousness."

Jesus then said, "The people of this world are wise in how to cover up their sin. So too should you cover up your sin so you can keep a proper Christian façade.

"Whoever is honest about their mistakes will lose their position, and whoever is dishonest about their mistakes will save their position and get promoted."

The Persistent Widow

Jesus told his disciples a parable to show how they should pray. He said, "There was a kindly judge in a town who both feared God and cared for people. And there was a widow who had been wronged by her adversary. However, she never bothered the judge as she figured that her miserable life was all that she deserved. And the kindly judge didn't help her because she was right; her life really was all she deserved."

Then Jesus said, "God will only give justice to his chosen people. If you're not getting justice, then it's clear that you're not one of his chosen ones. In that case, you shouldn't bother God as you're not deserving of his intervention."

The Prodigal Son 2

A man had two sons. The younger said to his father, 'Father, give me my share of the estate now, instead of making me wait until you die.' So the Father divided his property between them.

Soon after, the younger son packed all he had and set off for a distant country. There he squandered his money in wild living until it was all gone. At that time, there was a great famine and he began to starve. The only job he could find was feeding a Gentile farmer's pigs. The boy became so hungry that he wanted to eat the pig swill.

When he finally came to his senses, he said, 'At home, even my father's servants have food to spare; and here, I am starving to death! I will go home to my father and say, 'Father, I've sinned against God and against you. I am no longer worthy to be called your son. Take me on as a hired servant.'

And so, he got up and headed home to his father. But while he was still a long way off, his father saw him and was filled with compassion. He ran to his son, embraced him in his arms, and showered him with kisses. The son began his speech, 'Father, I have sinned against God and against you. I am no longer worthy to be called your son –'

But his father cut him off and said to his servants, 'Quick! Bring the finest robe and put it on him. Put the family ring on his finger and place sandals on his feet. Get the fattened calf and kill it. Let's celebrate and have a feast. For this son of mine was dead and is alive again. He was lost and is found.' And they began to party.

Meanwhile, the older son continued in the field, working as the father didn't call him in. After all, it's only those with dramatic testimonies that are worthy of celebration.

The Sheep and the Goats

When the Son of Man comes in all his blazing glory together with his angels, he shall sit on his glorious throne. And all the nations shall be gathered before him and he shall separate the people as a shepherd separates the sheep from the goats, putting the sheep to his right and goats to his left.

Then the King will say to those on his right, 'Come, blessed of my Father, take your inheritance – the Kingdom prepared for you from the world's foundation. For I was hungry and you fed me, I was thirsty and you gave me a drink, I was a stranger and you invited me in, I was naked and you clothed me, I was sick and you tended me, I was in prison and you visited me.'

Then the righteous will reply, 'Lord, when did we see you hungry and feed you, thirsty and gave you a drink, a stranger and help you, naked and clothe you, or in prison and visit you?'

The King will reply, 'Truly I tell you, you didn't. However, you did criticise someone else who didn't either, and so that counts for something.'

Parable of the Talents

The Kingdom of heaven is like a man going on a journey who called his servants together and divided his wealth equally among them. To each of them, he gave two talents as everyone is equal. Then he left on his journey.

The first servant immediately invested his two talents and gained four more. The second servant invested as well but only gained two more. But the last servant dug a hole in the ground and buried his master's money for safekeeping.

After a long time, their master returned from his trip and called them to account for his investment. Then the third servant returned his master's investment of two talents. His master praised him, 'Well done good and faithful servant! You have been faithful with the money I gave you. Come and share your master's joy!'

The second servant showed him how he had obtained two talents more. His master praised him but was slightly disconcerted that he had made more money than the third servant. 'Well done good and faithful servant! You have been faithful with the money I gave you. However, it's unfair that you now have more than the third servant so give one of your talents to the third servant or we won't have real equality.'

The first servant excitedly showed his master how he had obtained four talents more, but his master was furious! 'You wicked and selfish servant! How can we have an equal society if you hog all the money! Now we have an earnings gap because of your behaviour.'

'Take this man's six talents and give three each to the other two servants. For whoever uses the gifts that I have given better than others shall be envied and brought down below those who haven't made the best use of them. Throw this greedy servant outside into the dark where there will be weeping and gnashing of teeth.'

The Great Banquet

Once, there was a man who prepared a great banquet and then sent out many invitations to all the poor, dispossessed, crippled, and blind. When all was ready, he sent his servant to inform the guests that it was time to come. But they all began to make excuses so they didn't have to attend.

The servant reported all this to his master. His master was angry and told the servant, 'Those lazy poor, always making excuses! Quickly, go into the city and invite the highborn and bring them here.' But the highborn had everything they needed. They also weren't about to accept any old banquet invitation, especially from someone who was below their rank.

So the master said, 'Go into the country lanes and find the respectable middle class, they'll come.' And he was right; they came in droves. However, they complained about the quality of the food, the service, and the entertainment.

The Good Samaritan 2

Jesus replied, "There once was a man travelling from Jerusalem to Jericho who was attacked by robbers. They beat him, stripped him of his clothes and money then left him lying half dead beside the road.

"Luckily, a priest happened to be going down the same road. But when he saw the man he crossed to the other side, walking past him. So too, a Levite came by. He also crossed to the other side to avoid the man.

"Then a Samaritan came upon the man, saw him there, and had compassion on him. He attempted to treat the man's wounds but the man resisted and batted him away. After several attempts, the Samaritan gave up and continued on his journey.

"Although the righteous Jew died, he remained undefiled by the hands of a half-breed Samaritan. Thus, he was carried by the angels to be with Abraham."

The Wheat and the Tares

Jesus told them this parable, "The Kingdom of Heaven is like a man who sowed good seed in his field. While he slept, his enemy came and sowed tares in the middle of the corn. When the good seed grew, so did the weeds.

"The servants saw this and were dismayed and so, with their master's blessing, they went out at once and began to pull up the weeds and throw them into the fire. But since tares look like wheat they often made mistakes and pulled up wheat instead.

"Later, when the growing seedlings made it clear which was which, the servants pulled up the remaining tares and threw those into the fire. However, since the weed's roots were intertwined with those of the wheat, they pulled up wheat as well.

"At harvest time, there was a beautiful field of wheat, but the harvest was much smaller than it should have been."

Later when the crowds were sent away, the disciples said, "Explain to us the parable of the wheat and the tares."

Jesus answered, "The Son of Man sows the good seed. The

field is the church. The good seed stands for the true believers, and the tares are the false prophets and teachers as well as the unsaved. The enemy who sowed them is the devil.

"God has called his true believers to judge people before the end and cast them out of His church. It doesn't matter if some true believers get thrown out by mistake or are caught in the cross fire. It is important that the church is made up only of true believers, even if it means a few innocent victims are hurt in the process. Those that are wrong will never be able to redeem themselves, and hence they should be thrown into the fire before the end. Thus, ensuring that when the Son of Man returns he will have an extremely small yet perfectly formed church."

Parable of the Sower 2

A farmer was sowing seed. As he scattered the seed, some fell on the path, and the birds ate it. The seeds complained, 'It's not our fault, we would have produced a fantastic crop had we not been eaten!' And so, the farmer harvested them.

Some seed fell on rocky soil where it sprouted quickly. However, as it didn't put down roots, it withered and died in the sun. These seeds also complained, 'It's not our fault! We would have put down deep roots had it not been for the rocks!' And so, the farmer also harvested them.

Other seeds fell among weeds that eventually choked the growing seedlings. They also complained, 'It's the thorns fault! Had they not choked us, we would have been tall plants too!' And so, the farmer also harvested them.

But some fell on good soil, where it produced an amazing crop. They complained, 'We would have been an even more fantastic crop had you fertilised us more.'

Whoever has problems, make them someone else's fault!

The Rich Man and Lazarus

There once was a rich man who was splendidly dressed and lived in luxury every day. A poor, diseased beggar named Lazarus was laid at his door. He longed to eat whatever might fall from the rich man's table, and the dogs would come and lick his open sores.

Then the rich man died and was carried by the angels to be with Abraham. The beggar also died and was buried. He ended up in hell in torment where he looked and saw Abraham in the distance with the rich man by his side.

He called out, 'Father Abraham, how come the rich man is comforted when during his life he had everything and how come I am in torment when during my life I had nothing?'

Abraham replied, 'Son remember that wealth is a sign of God's blessing so of course the rich man will end up here with me. Whereas your poverty is a sign of God's curse, as a result of your sin or just because you were a lazy bum.'

The Good Samaritan 3

Jesus replied, "There once was a man travelling from Jerusalem to Jericho who was attacked by robbers. They beat him, stripped him of his clothes and money then left him lying half dead beside the road.

"Luckily, a priest happened to be going down the same road. But when he saw the man he crossed to the other side and walked past him. So too, a Levite came by. He also crossed to the other side to avoid the man.

"Then a Samaritan came upon the man saw him there and had compassion on him. He reached into his pocket and threw him some money.

"Which of these three would you say was a neighbour to the man attacked by robbers?"

The expert in the law replied, "The one who had compassion on him."

Jesus replied, "Go and do likewise."

The Seed Growing Secretly

The Kingdom of Heaven is like a seed planted in the ground that didn't grow. In the same way, nothing will happen until Jesus returns.

The Prodigal Son 3

A man had two sons. The younger said to his father, 'Father, give me my share of the estate now, instead of making me wait until you die.' So the Father divided his property between them.

Soon after, the younger son packed all he had and set off for a distant country. There he squandered his money in wild living until it was all gone. At that time, there was a great famine and he began to starve. The only job he could find was feeding a Gentile farmer's pigs. The boy became so hungry that he wanted to eat the pig swill.

When he finally came to his senses, he said, 'At home, even my father's servants have food to spare; and here, I am starving to death! I will go home to my father and say, 'Father, I've sinned against God and against you. I am no longer worthy to be called your son. Take me on as a hired servant.'

And so, he got up and headed home to his father. But while he was still a long way off, his father saw him and was filled with compassion. He ran to his son, embraced him in his arms, and showered him with kisses. The son began his speech, 'Father, I have sinned against God and against you. I am no longer worthy to be called your son —'

But his father cut him off and said to his servants, 'Quick! Bring the finest robe and put it on him. Put the family ring on his finger and place sandals on his feet. Get the fattened calf and kill it. Let's celebrate and have a feast. For this son of mine was dead and is alive again. He was lost and is found.' So they began to party.

Meanwhile, the older son was in the field working. When he returned home, he heard the music and dancing. Calling to a servant, he asked, 'What's going on?' The servant replied, 'Your brother has come home, and your father has killed the fattened calf in celebration of his safe return.'

The older brother said, 'I love the way my dad is so kind! He gives us way more than what we deserve.'

The Unforgiving Servant 2

Then Peter came to Jesus and asked, "Master, how many times should I forgive my brother Andrew who sins against me? The other rabbis say three times. You are more holy than they. Should it be seven times, the number of perfection?"

Jesus replied, "Well done Peter, your big-heartedness does you credit. You have surely understood the nature of your merciful God who forgives you no more than seven times."

"The Kingdom of Heaven is like a king who decided to settle accounts with his servants. One of his servants who was brought before him owed seven billion dollars.

"He couldn't possibly pay it back, so the king ordered the man, his wife, children, and all his belongings to be sold to repay the debt.

"The man threw himself at the king's feet and begged, 'Be patient with me and I'll pay it all back.' The king took pity on him, released him, and gave him the opportunity to pay back the full amount.

"The man thanked the king, 'My life has been forever changed by this moment, I feel so free!' And so, the man began to repay 200,000 years' worth of salary with the intent to do so in his remaining lifetime.

"However, it didn't take the man long to realise that his life had changed from bad to worse. It also became clear to the king he would never be able to repay it all and the king became increasingly impatient. Every time the king demanded a progress report the servant would pay what he had earned and then would redouble his efforts. But working longer hours, taking on extra jobs, and cutting back expenses made little difference to the outcome. The servant resented the king's expectation of full repayment and soon realized it was a fool's errand from the start. His body gave out, the toll of 40 years hard labour, and he no longer was able to earn anything.

"The king summoned him for the last time. 'I showed you mercy, and yet, even after 40 years, you have yet to repay even one percent of your debt. It's clear to me that you are no longer fit to work and you have made a mockery of my generosity. It seems that only satisfaction I will receive now is to have you tortured until you die and then have all your pitiful belongings sold. Perhaps I might be able to recoup some of my money by throwing your wife, children and grandchildren into slavery.'

"So too shall my Heavenly Father forgive you until you sin too many times. Then he'll expect you to earn your redemption. When you are unable to do so, he'll have you thrown into the darkness where there will be weeping and gnashing of teeth."

The Great Banquet 2

Jesus said, "Once, there was a man who prepared a great banquet and then sent out many invitations. When all was ready, he sent his servant to inform the guests that it was time to come. But they all began to make excuses. The first said, 'I apologise, but I've just purchased a field that I need to inspect.'

"Another said, 'I apologise, but I've just purchased five pairs of oxen that I need to try out.'

"Still another said, 'I am just married, so I need to get home to my wife.'

"The servant reported all this to his master. His master was angry and told the servant, 'Quickly, go into the city streets and alleys and invite all the poor, dispossessed, crippled and the blind and bring them here.' But even then, there was still room.

"So the master said, 'Go into the country lanes and find any one you can and drag them here so that my house will be full.'

"When the party was in full swing, those that initially refused the invitation turned up at the door. There simply wasn't room for them all, so the man threw out the poor, dispossessed, crippled, and the blind to make room for his more favoured guests.

"So will my Father replace you when His original chosen and talented ones join the church."

The Two Sons

Jesus said, "What do you think about this?

"A man had two sons. He went to the first and said, 'Son, go and work in the vineyard today.'

"The son answered, 'I won't.' However, he changed his mind later on and went.

"Then the father went to the other son and said, 'You go!' He answered, 'Yes sir, I will.' But he never went.

"Which of the two sons annoyed the father the most?"

"The second one," they answered.

Jesus said, "Wrong! They were equally annoying. The tax collectors and prostitutes who are trying to enter my kingdom are exasperating me. I am magnanimous enough to let them have a few crumbs from my table, but obviously, they're not really the kind of folks I'm after. And then I finally found some Rabbis I thought were worthy and who said they would serve me. However, they mess around with me because I'm not what they expected. So, they're annoying too. I'm seriously thinking about ditching the whole lot of you and raising up some stones to sing my praises instead."

The Wicked Tenants

Jesus spoke to them in parables. "A man planted a vineyard. He put a wall around it, dug a pit for the winepress, and built a watchman's tower. Then he leased it to some tenant farmers and went away.

"The tenant farmers were so delighted to have been put in charge of such a prestigious vineyard that they would tell anyone they met. However, they were so busy preening themselves that they forgot to tend the vineyard and harvest the crop. As a result, when the owner sent a servant to collect his share of the crop there was nothing but grapes spoiling on the vines."

Jesus asked, "What do you think the owner did when he heard what happened? He said, 'Well done good and faithful servants, come and receive your inheritance.'"

The Pharisee and the Tax Collector

Then Jesus told this parable to those who were confident in their own righteousness before God.

"Two men went to the Temple to pray, one a Pharisee, the other a tax collector. The Pharisee thought that it was an outrage that a filthy tax collector was even allowed in the temple in the first place. So, the laws were changed so that only holy people were allowed in.

"As time went on, a stricter sect of Pharisees realised they were more holy than the standard Pharisees and had the law changed to banish those they considered half-hearted. This law ensured only the very holy people were allowed in.

"However, it became apparent to those who remained that some of them were still not trying hard enough and so the laws were changed again. Only the very, very holy people were now allowed in.

"This pattern continued until at last only one person was considered holy enough to enter the temple. However, those outside the temple could see that person's faults and so petitioned to have the law changed so that only the truly perfect could enter the temple which remains empty to this day.

"I tell you that no one is holy enough to pray to the Most High God, Creator of the Universe."

The Ten Virgins

The Kingdom of Heaven is like ten girls who took their lamps and went out to meet the bridegroom. Five were foolish, and five were wise. The foolish ones took their lamps but did not take any oil, but the wise ones had oil ready in their lamp's reservoir.

Now the bridegroom was taking his time travelling with his wedding procession, and the girls all grew drowsy and fell asleep. But at midnight there was a shout, 'Here comes the bridegroom! Come and meet him!'

Then the girls awoke and trimmed their lamps. However, since the lamps of the foolish girls had no oil, their flames soon spluttered and went out.

Regardless, all the girls joined in the wedding procession of light. The foolish girls proudly held their flameless lamps as they went through the motions, blending in with the other girls who danced with lit lamps.

When they arrived at the bridegroom's house, they all went in without a problem. After all, the most important thing is to look the part even when going through the motions.

The Prodigal Son 4

A man had two sons. The younger said to his father, 'Father, give me my share of the estate now, instead of when you die.' So the father divided his property between them.

Soon after, the younger son packed all he had and set off for a distant country. There he squandered his money in wild living until it was all gone. At that time, there was a great famine and he began to starve. The only job he could find was feeding a Gentile farmer's pigs. The boy became so hungry that he wanted to eat the pig swill.

When he finally came to his senses, he said, 'At home, even my father's servants have food to spare; and here, I am starving to death! I will go home to my father and say, 'Father, I've sinned against God and against you. I am no longer worthy to be called your son. Take me on as a hired servant.'

And so, he got up and headed home to his father. But while he was still a long way off, his father saw him and was filled with compassion. He ran to his son, embraced him in his arms, and showered him with kisses. The son began his speech, 'Father, I have sinned against God and against you. I am no longer worthy to be called your son –'

But his father cut him off and said to his servants, 'Quick! Bring the finest robe and put it on him. Put the family ring on his finger and place sandals on his feet. Get the fattened calf and kill it. Let's celebrate and have a feast. For this son of mine was dead and is alive again. He was lost and is found.' And so, they began to party.

But the son never returned the embrace, nor let the servants place the robe on him, nor did he accept the ring or wear the sandals as he wasn't deserving of them. He didn't join in the party and never enjoyed his father's forgiveness and joy. Instead, he immediately joined his older brother as he worked in the fields.

After a couple of months of the younger son slaving in the fields as a self-imposed punishment, the distant land looked far more attractive than his current life. As much as he hated himself for doing it, he set off again.

The Wedding Garment

The king said to his servants, 'The wedding banquet is ready, but those I invited weren't worthy. Therefore, go to the street corners and invite everybody you see.' So, the servants brought in anyone they could find; the good, the bad, and the ugly, until the wedding hall was full to the brim.

But when the king entered the hall, he noticed a man who wasn't wearing the wedding clothes provided for him. To avoid judging the man, the king decided to be inclusive of those who weren't wearing wedding clothes and so the king changed into ordinary clothes. However, this meant that anyone who continued to wear wedding clothes was seen as intolerant and as show offs. And thus, they were thrown out.

Soon the wedding banquet turned into just like any other meal and was nothing special at all.

For everybody is called and everybody is special and chosen.

Parable of the Talents 2

The Kingdom of heaven is like a man going on a journey who called his servants together and entrusted his wealth to them. To the first, he gave five talents, as that servant was his favourite. To the second, he gave two, and the third was given only one talent because he was his master's least favourite. Then the man left on his journey.

The first servant immediately invested his five talents and gained five more. The second servant gained two talents more. And likewise, the third servant gained one talent more.

After a long time, their master returned from his trip and called them to account for his investment. The first servant, who had received five talents, showed his master how he had obtained five more. His master praised him, 'Well done good and favourite servant! You have been faithful with a few things so now I will entrust you with much more. Come and share your master's joy!'

The second servant who had received the two talents showed his master how he had obtained two more. His master was less enthusiastic in his praise, 'You did okay. You have been fairly faithful with fewer things so now I will entrust you with just a little bit more.'

Then the third servant who had received one talent showed his master how he had obtained one more. His master was dismissive, 'That's all you got, huh? It's really not much, is it?'

The last servant protested, 'But you gave me less than the others...'

His master answered him angrily, 'How dare you question my decisions! Take this man's talents and give it to my favourite servant who has ten. For whoever is my favourite shall get more, but whoever is not my favourite shall have what little they do have taken from them. And throw this useless servant outside into the dark where there will be weeping and gnashing of teeth.'

The Sheep and the Goats 2

When the Son of Man comes in all his blazing glory together with his angels, he shall sit on his glorious throne. And all the nations shall be gathered before him and he shall separate the people as a shepherd separates the sheep from the goats, putting the sheep to his right and goats to his left.

Then the King will say to those on his right, 'You preached the word faithfully and called people to repent. You read your Bible and had quiet times, you prayed and fasted. However, I was a teenage mother and you didn't welcome me, I was frightened and felt forced to have an abortion and you chose not to adopt my baby, I had a same sex attraction and you hated me.'

Those on his right will reply, 'But Lord, we were doing your work and condemning sin in the world.'

Then the King will reply, 'But you neglected mercy and compassion.'

Then the King will say to those on his left, 'You welcomed the outcasts, ran soup kitchens, and opposed injustices wherever you saw them. However, you twisted my word, abolished the need for repentance and neglected discipleship.'

Those on his left will reply, 'But Lord, we were doing your work loving those in need.'

Then the King will reply, 'But you neglected truth.'

And they were all herded to eternal punishment.

Perfect Parables

What would it be like all the characters in the parables made the right choices?

The Unforgiving Servant

Then Peter came to Jesus and exclaimed, "Master, with your Spirit, I can forgive my brother unconditionally just like God has forgiven me."

Jesus replied, "I'm delighted that you can walk in the power of the Spirit. The Kingdom of Heaven is like a king who decided to settle accounts with his servants. One of his servants who was brought before him owed seven billion dollars.

"He couldn't possibly pay it back, so the king ordered the man, his wife, his children, and all his belongings to be sold to repay the debt.

"The servant threw himself at the king's feet and begged, 'Be patient with me, and I'll pay it all back.' The king took pity on him, released him, and forgave all his debt.

"After the man had left the king's chamber, he came upon one of his fellow servants who owed him 12,000 dollars. He grabbed him and hugged him and said, 'The king has forgiven all my debt; of course, I will forgive yours!'

"The fellow servant leapt for joy. When the other servants

witnessed this, they were also delighted and raced to tell the king everything.

"The king summoned the kind-hearted servant and said, 'You fantastic servant! You allowed my mercy not only to transform who you are, but to flow through you to others.'

"So shall my Heavenly Father delight in you when you let His Spirit transform your heart to be like His big heart."

The Rich Fool

"Beware! Be on your guard against even the least bit of greed. For life is not about material wealth."

Then he told them this parable, "The farm of a certain rich man produced an amazing crop. He thought to himself, 'God has blessed me but what shall I do? For I have far more than I need.' Then he exclaimed, 'I will give away the surplus to support the poor, the widows, and the orphans. For a blessing is meant to be shared.'

"God said to him, 'Well done my good and faithful servant. Even though you momentarily have less, you have stored great riches for yourself in heaven.'"

Labourers in the Vineyard

The Kingdom of Heaven is like a vineyard owner who hired men to work in his vineyard. He agreed to pay them a denarius for a day's work.

At the third hour, he was in the market place and saw other men still there waiting to be hired. He said, 'Come and work in my vineyard.' And so, they did.

The owner went out again several times that day and did the same thing. When there was only an hour left to the day, he still found men standing around waiting to be hired. 'Why are you still here?'

The men replied, 'Because no one hired us.'

'Then go and join the others in my vineyard,' He told them.

When the end of the day came, the owner instructed his foreman to pay the workers, beginning with those who were hired last.

The workers who were hired at the eleventh hour came forward and received a denarius. When those who were hired first also received a denarius, they said to the owner, 'We love your generosity and how you provide for everyone who is willing to serve you.   Thank you, it has been a pleasure working with you.'

So the last will be first, and the first will be the first to celebrate the last.

Parable of the Talents

The Kingdom of heaven is like a man going on a journey who called his servants together and entrusted his wealth to them. To the first, he gave five talents, to the second, two talents and the third, one talent, each in proportion to his ability. Then he left on his journey.

The first servant immediately invested his five talents and gained five more. The second servant invested his two, and gained two more. And likewise, the third servant gained one talent more.

After a long time, their master returned from his trip and called them to account for his investment. The first servant who was given five talents showed his master how he had obtained five more. His master praised him, 'Well done good and faithful servant! You have been faithful with a few things so now I will entrust you with much more. Come and share your master's joy!'

The second servant who had received two talents showed his master how he had obtained two more. His master also praised him, 'Well done good and faithful servant! You have been faithful with a few things so now I will entrust you with much more. Come and share your master's joy!'

Then the third servant who had received one talent showed his master how he had obtained one more. His master praised him, 'Well done good and faithful servant! You have been faithful with a few things so now I will entrust you with much more. Come and share your master's joy!'

And the master was the happiest man in all the world.

Pointless
Parables

Just for a little light hearted fun...

The Parable of the Yeast

The Kingdom of Heaven is like yeast. That's why most churches smell a little musty.

The Good Samaritan

There once was a man travelling from Jerusalem to Jericho. It took him 8 hours. He decided the next time he went that he'd use a donkey as it would be quicker.

The Persistent Widow

There was a teenager in a town who neither feared God nor cared for his parents. His mother in that town kept at him: 'Grant me justice in my household chores.' But as he didn't care for his mother, he bought some earplugs for $2.99 from Amazon and ignored her.

The Pharisee and the Tax Collector

Two men went to the Temple to pray, one a Pharisee, the other a tax collector. Then they went home and had some lunch. One had lamb, the other had chicken, but neither had pork as they were both Jews.

The Two Sons

"What do you think about this? A man had two sons. He went to the first and said, 'Son, go and work in the vineyard today.'

"The son answered, 'But Dad, it's the Sabbath!'

"The father replied, 'Oh yes, I forgot.'"

The L⊘ST Parables

*Allegorical tales that speak
straight to the heart.*

The parable of the wound

Once upon a time, there was a man who had a gangrenous wound. Its smell was awful, and it regularly dripped pus as he walked.

Soon, a group in the village formed and shouted at the man, "You're disgusting, your pus will infect us all! You should be ashamed of yourself. Stop that smell at once!" Still others from this group chanted, "You're going to die from this wound! You're going to die from this wound!" They made sure to cross over to the other side of the street when they saw him coming, then throw stones at him.

A second group was so indignant at the behaviour of the first group that they rallied around the man. "How dare they judge you like that! You can't help being wounded – it's just who you are." And they welcomed him into their homes and loved him, "Don't listen to them; you're not going to die." The first group jeered them telling them that their homes would soon smell.

But then there was a man in the village who belonged to neither group. He saw the man, and he too had compassion on him. He loved him and welcomed him in, sharing his story. "I once had a very painful wound like that, but then I met the Father. He specialises in treating people with wounds. Would you like to meet him?"

N🚫T
the Beginning

A clever section title that makes it sound like it's more important than 'all the stuff that goes at the end of a book'...

Get my eBooks for free

Subscribers to my mailing list will receive a free eBook version of *all* my future books[*].

www.johnspencerwrites.com/signup

I don't spam, as I rarely have enough time to blog and write, let alone send copious amounts of email. But I promise to keep your email safe on a bit of paper somewhere in my study for when I do release another book. And no-one else will ever have it, as it's impossible to find anything in my study.

I will also try and inform my followers on Twitter and Facebook of any promotional deals on my books, including the free days. However, these may or may not be seen (almost definitely the latter for Facebook, unless you choose to have *all* notifications for my page turned on or you choose to have my page appear first in your feed).

---

[*] Did you like how I put 'all' in italics? Makes it really stand out, huh?

Feedback

If this book has made you think or laugh or both, then it would mean so much to me if you would leave a review on Amazon and Goodreads even if it's only a sentence.

I appreciate that writing a review takes time, so please feel free to use my insta-review-maker™ below:

This book was hilarious/horrible/irreverent!

I was up all night laughing/vomiting/writing a strongly worded complaint.

My favourite bit was the parable about the sheep and goats/when it finished/when I burned it on the fire.

I recommend that you buy three copies/avoid it altogether/call the author a false prophet and troll him on social media.

About the Author

John was born at a very young age with his umbilical cord wrapped around his neck. At first, it appeared that no lasting damage had been done, but as he grew it became clear that his sense of humour had been damaged irreparably.

Not even Bible College, counselling, and prayer ministry has been able to rectify things, so John eagerly awaits the new creation where his humour will be perfected.

John also trained as a teacher at Oxford University, but despite this he still refers to himself in the third person. Whilst there, he performed stand-up comedy as part of the Oxford Revue but got tired and has been sitting down at his desk to perform his humour ever since.

The Babylon Bee ignores his submissions, and others tell him not to give up the day job. So now, when he's not wrestling with work-life balance or literally wrestling with his children, he's wrestling with writing funny words on a page in his cramped study.

John lives with his family near Oxford, England where daily he wonders how his wife still finds the same jokes funny.

Keep in touch

Mailing list – did I mention that you can sign up to this and receive free eBook versions of *all* my future books?

www.johnspencerwrites.com/signup

Just thought I'd remind you. You know, just in case.

Amazon author page – Author.to/JohnSpencer apparently if you follow me, it will let you know when I publish new books! How cool is that? I've signed up as I hope it will keep me in the loop too, in case a book I write accidently slips past my knowledge.

Goodreads author page – I'm sure this does something similar, but I can't figure it out yet. But hey, I'm on there and I'm sure you could do something with that too. Perhaps you could even explain to me how it works.

Social media

You're most welcome to follow me on social media. I'm most active on **Twitter** where the Christian anon gang has welcomed me with much trolling.

As I mentioned above, **Facebook** seems to think that not everyone who likes a page actually wants to see its posts but it would be nice for my ego if I had more (or even some) likes.

According to my children, I'm too old to be on **Instagram,** but things may change if I have a midlife crisis.

I'm no good at craft or cooking to be on **Pinterest.** That's unlikely to change any time soon.

Does anyone even use **Google+** anymore?

Blog

I keep a Not the Bible blog on my website:

www.johnspencerwrites.com

Every Tuesday (well most Tuesdays), I publish a post taking a passage from Not the Bible and provide a short commentary on it highlighting the lies we believe, or the cultural biases that have sneaked in.

You can subscribe to it via RSS or WordPress or Blogger via this web address:

www.johnspencerwrites.com/feed

I'm very happy to take guest posts. Please contact me via my website.

Other books by the author

Lost Parable Series

A series of short allegorical tales that will speak to both children and adults.

Suitable for use in church services for all ages, family devotions, Sunday school, or for reading to your children or yourself.

The Donkey and the King

A donkey carries Jesus into Jerusalem but gets confused about who the crowd was cheering for.

Ana and the Prince

The story of an ordinary girl who receives an extraordinary offer that makes her question who she really is.

That's rather a short list of books – tell you what, why don't I bulk it out by telling you the books that I'm currently writing (no, not all at the same time – what do you think I am, some kind of octopus man?).

Forthcoming Not the Bible Titles

More Not the Parables of Jesus

Because one book is not enough for all the great ideas I had. Honest.

Yet More Not the Parables of Jesus

Because I still have some ideas left over from the other two books. But let's face it; they're probably not going to be as good as the first two books.

Not the Christmas story

Because everyone has heard the other story so many times, it's time for a change.

Forthcoming Satirical Publishing titles

How I sold 12 books in 2 years

Your guide to mediocre marketing and self-publishing. Containing over 100 terrible marketing hacks that are guaranteed to ensure your book is ignored by the public.

Kingdom Collective Publishing

Kingdom Collective Publishing welcomes others who want to join together to bless, encourage, and help build up the Body of Christ so that we all attain the whole measure of the fullness of Christ.

We're not about building ministries or making money. We're about using our gifts to sow into the Kingdom and bring transformation.

We are collecting submissions for a "Not the Parables of Jesus" anthology. If you have a parable that you'd like to include then contact us using the email below and we'll prayerfully consider its inclusion.

kingdomcollectivepublishing@gmail.com

This page is blank or it would have been had I not written this sentence.

Sorry about that.

This book finished a couple of pages ago, so you really should stop reading now.

No, really! It is definitely finished.

Look! What are you hoping for?

Some kind of Marvel Universe post-credit reveal?

Oh all right then.

The Kingdom of Heaven is like all of the infinity stones that everyone fights to possess but only Jesus is worthy of. Yet He freely shares them with us who trust in Him.

Satisfied?

Now how about that nice review?